CRICKET ... REAL CRICKET

Malcolm R. Stratton

Slasher of note!
1MM men out!

Best wishes,

George.

Also by the same author:

TALES FROM THE TIN TABERNACLE

Further Tales
from the Tin Tabernacle

by

George Andrew

DARF PUBLISHERS LIMITED
London
1989

© Copyright Darf Publishers Ltd
London 1989

FIRST PUBLISHED 1989

Cartoons drawn by: Ray Griffiths

ISBN 1 85077 210 X

Printed in Great Britain by BPCC Wheatons Ltd, Exeter

Contents

Further Tales from the Tin Tabernacle	*Page*
Foreword	7
The Tales of Winston and the 'Incredible Snowman'	11
New Year's Day. Review and Resolutions	25
Indoor Nets. 'Bats' and 'Aerobics'	31
The Indoor League. An 'Irresistible Force' meets an 'Immovable Object'	37
The 'Glory Hole'	45
'Marrieds' v. 'Singles'	51
Venez a 'Plus Frappez Par Le Seule'	67
The Visit of the Touring Celebrity side	69
The Ultimate in Local Derbies	75
The Annual Dinner Dance	89

Foreword

Geoff, the captain, continues to lead his mixed band from "Much Sloggin' by the Willow Cricket Club" through a new season. Why this should start on 26th December is a matter of honour, although this has little to do with Winston's manipulation of the result.

Piers ffrenche-epistle grows in stature, proving the graffiti on the Ladies' loo to be inaccurate. He can also be found in prayer when an 'Irresistible Force' meets an 'Immovable Object'.

Lobby makes his debut as captain, leading the 'Singles' against the 'Marrieds' in a match that has little to do with matrimony.

Two newcomers join the team; 'Dinger' Bell, from New Zealand, dentist and number three bat; 'Rabbit On' Reggie, clothed by Ox-Fam, destined for Drama School and a fast bowler of unusual style.

The Final of the Hospital Memorial Knock-Out Cup ends in a nail-biting finish and the year draws to a close at the Dinner Dance as Tallulah and Carole reveal the secret of the 'Autographed Bat'.

CHAPTER ONE

The tale of Winston and the 'Incredible Snowman'

It is the day after Christmas. Boxing Day. What, you may ask has this to do with cricket? Let me take you back two months.

A challenge was issued by the football club on the occasion of their defeat, at soccer, by four goals to one, for a return fixture . . . playing cricket. The bar had run out of both draught Guiness and bottled Newcastle Brown Ale, the night was late and brains not functioning at their normal half power.
"When do you want to play then?" Geoff was keen, secure in the knowledge that his 'strategy', which had worked so well in the football match, could be used to good effect against a joke team.
"Well. It's now the 23rd of October, we'd better make it this year. What about Boxing Day, proceeds to go to charity?"
Nathaniel the groundsman turned a whiter shade of lambswool and attempted to get to his feet.
"You're on," said Geoff. "We can put the practice mat down so it doesn't matter what the weather's like."
Winston, the social secretary, insisted that due solemnity be given to the acceptance. It was recorded in the 'Wagers Book' which was kept behind the bar and those members of both teams still present drank a special toast to seal the agreement.
Toast was the appropriate word since glasses of Sambuca Dei Cesari were poured, then set alight with a reverence the Ancient Druids would have appreciated. The woad blue flames were then

"You don't mean you'd be put off by the weather, do you?"

admired before being blown out, prior to the warmed nectar being tipped down receptive throats. Lobby Lowslung made two mistakes. Due to the absence of his top teeth his attempt to blow out the flame missed, leaving the spirit still very much alight; he then put the glass to his bottom lip, where it attached itself with the tenacity of Instant Glue, while his magnificent moustache and sideboards illuminated the whole scene by catching fire.

Only prompt action by Ben saved the situation. With an abandon seldom seen before he threw his nearly full pint of heavy bitter at Lobby's head.

Boxing Day saw long queues outside the bookies. Having received their banker from the Weather Men, who had predicted a fine festive season, the locals had all confidently accepted the six to one offered on snow and had woken up on Christmas Day to find everywhere 'White Over'. An unbroken mantle some two inches deep covered the cricket pitch as the teams, clutching their glasses of Toddy, gazed towards the sacred square, identified by the sagging rope that looped round the edge.

"That's that, then," Ian, the football captain, turned back to the bar.

"What do you mean?" said Geoff, a grin appearing on his face. "You don't mean that you'd be put off by the weather do you?"

There was a long silence, then a roar of approval from the cricket team.

"Of course we'll play," said Ian. "Let's get the rules sorted out."

Geoff was taken aback by this. Laws of cricket, the local version, he was a master at manipulating. Football Club rules for charity matches were something new to him.

There was a liquid interlude while the two teams conferred. The football club's intellectual, Hacker Hargett, more of a stopper than a sweeper, was duly sat down and supplied with pen and paper. Geoff was worried by the amount of laughter which came from the group, and it was with some trepidation that he looked at the list Ian eventually pinned up on the notice board.

1. Eleven overs for each innings, one to be bowled by each member of the side.

"Service from the bar shall continue throughout the course of the game"

2. Service from the bar shall continue throughout the course of the game.

3. On the taking of a wicket, a tray containing thirteen half pints of mulled ale shall be carried to the players and umpires for their consumption.

4. The scoring of a four by a batsman shall be celebrated by the batsman drinking a half measure of ale. In the event of him hitting a six, his just reward shall be a pint of the aforesaid ale.

5. Drinks bill to be paid for at the end of the game by the losing side.

Addendum. As it is unlikely that there will be any fours scored, the umpires are empowered to judge whether a shot would have produced a four and signal accordingly.

Addendum addendum. Shorts shall be served to the two batsmen in residence when the score reaches double figures, and on every multiple of ten.

"Right," said Geoff. "Agreed. Downstairs to the changing room my side, for a tactical team talk."

The Cricket Club had prepared themselves well for the game. This became evident when they began to change. As the various items were donned there was a fashion parade the like of which had never, thankfully, been seen in the fashion houses of the world. Long, woollen, hairy garments enshrouded limbs. All the players dressed in a variety of long johns, ranging from the thermal silk of poseur Piers to the genuine red flannel of Ben. However good the cricket, the team were assured of remaining warm.

"What we've got to do is wrap this game up as soon as possible," began Geoff, "I want us back in the bar by four o'clock."

"It is also vital," said Winston, "that we win. Just think how much that drink bill is going to be. What's the strategy going to be today, Skipper?"

"First, and most important, we have got to win the toss."

"Well, that's no problem," said Piers, who had learned the lesson well, "I mean it's just a case of producing the coin first, making him call, then telling him he's lost without letting him see the coin."

"Then what," said Geoff. "Do we bat first or field?"

There was no shortage of immediate advice, the majority of the voices being raised in support of batting.

"Think about it," said Geoff. "First of all it means that you lot are quietly improving the bar profits from the comfort of the pavilion, while, hopefully, Nigel and Piers are scoring enough runs to win the game. Bearing in mind that if they're getting drinks for every four and chasers for every ten scored, we can write them off when it's time to field."

"And the opposition will be sober," said Nigel. "Assuming they don't take any wickets."

"But if we field first and take the ten wickets quickly," Richard the treasurer, was scrambling his brains with calculations. "That means that we'll have drunk five pints of mulled ale, which might impair our judgement when we come to bat."

"Especially if the football club are bringing the drinks, there's no telling what they might slip into them." Lobby was cautious, suspicious and experienced, having played in goal on one disastrous occasion.

"We'll bat," Geoff said. "Piers and Nigel you can bat until your innings is four drinks long, just in case we need you to bowl. The same applies to the rest of you. No heroics. You go in, push the score along by nineteen and then get yourselves out. Understood?"

Murmurings of agreement from the team as they completed their gladiatorial outfits.

"I shall also keep an eye on all of you in the bar. We don't want to sacrifice the glory of winning and substitute that for the ignominy of paying the drinks bill."

Pride cometh however, before the fall. Of the ten pence coin in this case, which disappeared below the snow and was found by Ian a good yard away from where it had fallen. Tails up, just as he had called.

"We'll bat," he said. "It's part of our strategy." He smiled and winked at Geoff. "Doesn't always work twice you know. Remember how you were so keen to kick downhill with the wind in the football match?"

The match began just after one o'clock, leaving some three hours of reasonable daylight.

Geoff decided that he'd intersperse his better bowlers with the totally useless ones, in order to create some space between the wickets falling and the trays of ale arriving. It was a tactic which might have worked if he hadn't then allowed Winston to take the new ball.

The pitch had never looked better. An island of green matting on a white sea. True the batsmen had to slip and slide their way to the wicket as they crossed the snow in their unspiked boots, but once there they could depend on being sure footed. To begin with at least.

Winston's first ball was, even to a regular batsman, a nightmare. A full bloodied Yorker, pitched right up on the toes, swinging in to the body and cutting back to demolish the stumps. Which it duly did, without the football club opener opening his eyes. 0 for 1, $13 \times \frac{1}{2}$ pint. The umpires smiled.

Geoff walked across to Winston, and put his arm round him.

"That was one of the best balls you've ever bowled," he said. "Don't do it again."

"But I'm on for a double hat trick," said Winston. "I can go straight through this lot."

"You do," said Geoff, "Winston, you do that and we won't be able to get the pads on our lot, let alone pass the total. Which will mean you buying four jugs for the hat tricks, and probably paying the challenge drinks bill as well."

"Why four jugs?" Winston was mystified.

"Think about it. One for the first three balls, one for balls two, three and four. One for three, four and five and one for four, five and six. Got it?"

Winston's brow furrowed, "Alright, Skipper, I'll take it easy. I promise I won't take a hat trick."

He was true to his word. The second ball was a gentle full toss which was despatched with total abandon to the region of the mid-wicket boundary, high in the air some five yards to the left of Piers. He took two faltering steps, lunged, slid, skidded nose first into a minor snow drift and ploughed his way into a beautifully executed ski turn. While the rest of the fielders collapsed in laughter the batsmen ran and slithered their way through five runs. Piers eventually emerged, threw the ball back and was awarded 5.7 for execution and 5.9 for style. The umpires conferred and decided, much to the disgust of the exhausted batsmen, that the stroke was

"I reckon he's a ringer"

worth four and signalled to the scorer safely ensconced in the pavilion. She swore a very unladylike oath, rubbed out the five she had credited to the number three batsman and substituted a four.

Double measures of Navy Rum were despatched to both the batsmen and the umpires.

Winston's third ball, being a delivery some considerable k.p.h. faster than the second, removed both the batsman's bat and stumps before he'd managed to complete any real resemblance to a back lift. Mulled ale, round two.

The football club number four, unrecognised by any of the cricket team, drove the next ball into the snow towards cover point, who waited until he could identify the track through the snow and then burrowed away until he found it. The batsman walked a gentle single.

"That," said Ben to Lobby, "that was a shot played by someone who has played the game before and knows what he's doing. Who is he?"

"I don't recognise him," said Lobby, "I've played for the football club (a look of pain fled across his face) and run the line for them many times. I reckon he's a 'Ringer'."

The next ball hit what must have been a lump of ice, flew past Lobby's astonished whiskers and ground to a halt some twenty yards behind him. The umpires signalled four byes; the football club added a further codicil to the rules and carried out a lighted Sambula for Lobby, who, remembering the previous occasion he'd set himself on fire, put out the flames with a glove full of snow and drank the ensuing sludge, in one.

The remaining opening batsman was unlucky. Winston's last ball lifted, a sign of the change that was beginning to take place in the matting, took a thick edge and stuck, to Lobby's amazement, to the snow in his gloves. Wicket and tray number three.

A brave soul from the football team rushed out of the pavilion and brought the scoreboard up to date.

```
RUNS . . . . . . . . . . . 9
WICKETS . . . . . . . . 3
LAST MAN . . . . . . . 0
OVERS . . . . . . . . . . 1
```

"... and to Lobby's amazement, stuck to the snow on his glove"

Geoff looked round, selected Ben and threw the ball to him. Ben hadn't bowled since 1957. It was an interesting and long over. Ben had difficulty getting his creaking shoulder to work and his arm high enough to stop the umpire calling no ball. That matter was resolved by Winston who took up a fielding position close, very close, to the official and talking to him in a low voice. What was said was never revealed but the umpire virtually disappeared as his red face turned white. The quality of the stranger was revealed as the football club's total accelerated to twenty-four.

Fortunes fluctuated throughout the rest of the innings. Winston wandered down to fine leg, alternated with a vague sort of mid-off on alternate overs and built a magnificent snowman almost as tall as himself. It played a significant part in the dismissal of the 'Ringer' who was tempted into a lofted drive at one of Pier's gentle off breaks. The ball stuck firmly in the snowman's chest. The umpires by this stage were convinced that it was a member of the fielding side and ignored the protests of the football club, which were partly mitigated by the fact that it was the last ball of the innings. The scoreboard set out the task in front of Geoff's team.

```
RUNS .......... 83
WICKETS ........ 8
LAST MAN ...... 41
OVERS ......... 11
```

The Cricket Club innings started disastrously and then got worse. After three overs the total stood at seventeen runs for four wickets. Lobby joined Geoff at the wicket and by keeping their heads down and avoiding the alcoholic extravagances of possible fours they pushed the score along steadily until, skating down the wicket to take a single, they collided in the middle of the wicket. They were initially both given out by the football club umpire until Bill intervened to explain that that was against the Laws, both of justice and cricket. Lobby departed to leave Geoff to take over the job of saving the game. A flurry of runs and snow saw the addition of another ten runs and the loss of three more wickets. Winston joined Geoff at the wicket, one over to go and the scoreboard recorded:

```
RUNS . . . . . . . . . . 67
WICKETS . . . . . . . . 8
LAST MAN . . . . . . . 3
OVERS . . . . . . . . . 10
```

"This is serious," said Winston, as he joined Geoff for a mid-wicket conference.

"I know, I know," said Geoff. "Seventeen to win off six balls."

"I'm talking about the drinks bill," said Winston. "It's already well into three figures."

"I have a plan," said Geoff. "Providing we can get close enough by the last ball, here's what we do." The voices lowered as they became aware of the fielding side getting closer.

Ian, the football club captain, had kept himself back for the final over. The first two balls lobbed high, hit Winston amidships, falling on him out of a blackening sky. The next, a yard short, vanished, suddenly reappearing in front of third man. The reason was the state of the wicket. A vicious decline in the temperature had turned the matting into a frozen skating rink, the ball pinged off this sheet of ice like a golf ball landing on concrete. Bill emulated a scarecrow, arms akimbo, then swept his arms violently from side to side, signalling four wides and attempting to warm himself at the same time.

"Four wides," he bellowed at the top of his voice, in case there was any doubt.

The pantomime was repeated off the next two balls. A hurried conference was called by the football team with Mac MacDonald coming up with a possible winning solution.

"Curling," he said. "Roll the ball along the ice."

"Is that legal?" Ian asked Bill, who was reluctantly forced to agree that Ian could bowl underarm if he declared it first.

"Right Winston, change of action, you're about to be torpedoed," Ian shouted, just as the sky suddenly decided to fall. Snowflakes the size of eyeballs began to obscure the whole field. The players, dressed in white, became ghost figures. Ian lined up on Winston, whose face gleamed in the whiteout. Three balls were 'curled' and stopped by Winston as the snow thickened and visibility became worse. The final ball was rolled gently down the snow-covered ice, delicately weighted to just reach the wicket keeper should it pass the bat.

Winston came forward in the classic 'Thou Shall Not Pass' stance, his feet shuffled, a huge blizzard of snow surrounding him as he shuffled forward.

"Run!" he called.

Which they did, turned and came back for a second, while the opposition frantically kicked away at the snow, slipping and sliding, falling over in an ever-growing heap in a desperate effort to find the ball.

The third and fourth runs were scampered but the fifth and sixth gently strolled before Bill called out:

"Lost ball. Six."

In the home team dressing room, Geoff and Winston stood looking at each other.

"Brilliant . . . brilliant," said Geoff. "Where is it?"

Winston plunged down the front of the bulk of vest, trousers and underwear with an enormous hand, which emerged clutching the missing ball.

Putting the kit away after they'd changed they were surprised to find that there were only five stumps.

The mystery was solved the following morning when it was found, giving a new meaning to the title 'The Incredible Snowman'.

CHAPTER TWO

New Year's Day.
Review and Resolutions

In which Geoff, Lobby, Roger and Winston look back over the past season, review the coming year and make the 'odd' Resolution.

The old year had gone out with one of the coldest nights of the decade. The party had seen the customary scenes of revelry, followed by a welter of cursing in the car park as vehicles were battered into starting by a mixture of brute force and expertise. The inside of the clubhouse had been left for the morning.

Geoff and Lobby arrived to find that to get in they had to use anti-freeze on the doorkey. The sight that greeted them was nearly enough to make them turn straight round. Half-eaten turkey sandwiches mixed with the tinsel, full ashtrays competed with empty glasses for space on the tables. The floor had to be crossed with care. Stepping over the debris Geoff and Lobby made their way to the multi-padlocked door to the bar. Inside they were greeted by a still life that could have been painted by Salvador Dali. Crates of soft drinks caught the eye immediately. The bottles sat in the crates, but the tops were balanced on long, extended elegant necks. The overnight temperature of minus twenty had caused the liquid to turn to ice. There was a new carpet glittering like the floor of Aladdin's cave where glass mixed with ice. Geoff turned to Lobby.

"The tops were balanced on long extended elegant necks"

"So much for the thermostat which is supposed to switch the heating on when the temperature plummets," he said.

"Probably frozen up," said Lobby. "I'll go and turn the gas heaters on."

Geoff unlocked the kitchen, filled and plugged in the kettle and took an assortment of brushes, buckets and black sacks through to the main room.

"We'd better have a coffee and wait for the others," he said. "They'll never believe it otherwise and we're going to need all four of us to check and confirm the damage."

Winston and Roger arrived, wrapped up against the arctic conditions. Once they'd thawed out the battle commenced. Two hours later the club had been restored to pristine perfection and the group were celebrating with a well-laced hot drink, seated round a table, sorting out the season to come.

"Well," said Geoff, "I think we've got a full fixture list for the first time for years. Plus a few special highlights. Like the Under Sixteen District game which we're hosting."

"I saw one of those last year," said Lobby. "The winning team left immediately after the game and then went round the corner, jumped into their cars and drove off to the nearest pub. Some very hefty under sixteens there."

"That's the organiser's problem, not ours," said Winston. "All we've got to do is provide a pitch, changing rooms and tea."

"Then there's the Indoor League," said Roger. "I'm looking forward to that. We should do well with our experience."

"Plus the County Side coming for the Benefit Match and Pieter van Schwarzwinkel has agreed to be guest speaker at the Dinner Dance," Geoff said. "I think we've got reason to be cautiously optimistic about the season."

"We're going to need some new players though. Piers was the only real find last year, and we lost Elvis."

"Talking of Piers," said Winston. "There's a new piece of graffiti in the Ladies Loo. Have you seen it?"

"Go on," said Roger, "you're the privileged person who got to clean it out this morning."

"It reads something like. 'Don't call him Piers, call him Justin'. Underneath someone else has written 'Why?' Then it finishes with, 'Because he's got such a little ...' and the last word's been scrubbed out."

"I wonder who found that out?" said Lobby, "I thought he was such a Vestal sort of person."

"Right," said Geoff. "Time we moved. Let's have one New Year Resolution each before we go."

"That's easy," said Lobby. "I'm going to resolve not to get married."

"That's not fair," said Winston. "No one would have you anyway. My resolution is that I'm going to stop deceiving my lady, Tallulah."

"How?" said Geoff.

"Well, you know we've established a 'Men's Night Out' every Friday, where we play darts and have a meat raffle. Tallulah's been happy for me to go because I win a chicken every week. It's sort of conditional on my going the following week that I come home with a different bird every time. It's a joke really."

"But you've never won anything in the meat raffle," said Lobby.

"I come home with a different bird every time"

"No, but I keep a supply of chickens in the club fridge and take one from there every week."

"What are you going to give up, Geoff? said Lobby.

"I think I'll make the ultimate concession and give up 'strategy'," replied the captain.

"You can't do that," said Winston, absolutely horrified. "We'd never win another match."

"And I'm going to give up drink"

"How about if I give it up on those occasions when it's not really necessary?" said Geoff.

"That'll do," said Roger, "I'm going to give up drink."

"Impossible," said Lobby. "Apart from which you're so bloody objectionable when you're sober."

"Alright then," said Roger, "I won't drink on the thirty-first of April, June, September and November."

CHAPTER THREE

Indoor Nets. 'Bats' and 'Aerobics'

The Ancient and Modern methods of continuing to punish the ball and the body when the days are short and the limbs are stiff.

In the past the club had booked, on the twins' recommendation, a 'space' for the winter sessions. There was certainly room. The area used was part of an old, unconverted hangar. Nets was a euphemism, they were conspicuous by their absence. A strip of coconut matting was put down on the splintering floor and nobody was allowed to bowl at full pace. Even so, Winston, off three paces, could be terrifying, especially if someone was foolish enough to upset him.

The only spectators were the bats, winged variety, high up in the rafters, and the caretaker. He stood at the doorway, cackling with laughter, until one night when a drive from Roger scored a direct hit on his knee and he was never seen again. The lighting consisted of unprotected sixty-watt bulbs dangling from long leads, but still high enough to be out of danger from all but the wildest of vertical swings.

There was a general air of gloom. Dust seemed to hang in the air, disturbed only momentarily by the passage of a ball. Even the wind, as it swept through the holes in the plaster, corrugated sheeting (that had been nailed on as a temporary measure during the war), made only minor whirls amongst the greyish mist.

Bill and Ben were the only ones who were really happy there. The reason was undoubtedly nostalgia, they were constantly smiling, remembering their wartime service in the R.A.F.

This year there was a complete contrast. Imagine an enormous Leisure Centre. The main hall, the size of a small football pitch, surrounded by viewing balconies, gleams a warning to any speck of dirt thinking of settling. Aluminium, dazzling white paint, polished wood and polished bodies. At one side there are two lanes of nets, immaculate. Twin tongues of new matting unfurl between the green, fishermen's paradise drapes. One avenue is in use, the figures running up to bowl in their turn, the batsmen stroking the ball with a restraint that reduces the crack of willow to a whisper.

Enter the Much Sloggin' by the Willow team. Clutching their ancient leather bag they unpack the gear; bats, pads and stumps that have seen better days and been relegated to the 'nets' bag. Unlike the gleaming red leather balls that are being used next to them, there are a selection of brown, white and even yellow practice balls that have been over-used and abandoned by hockey teams.

The footwear is also distinctive, ranging from a mixture of 'Tackies'; once known as plimsoles and probably dating from that era; to the carpet slippers that are Winston's concessions to the

"The footwear is also distinctive"

"A hundred and fifty nubile girls appeared"

request that 'Soft Shoes Will Be Worn At All Times'. The players are in a kaleidoscope of colours, not having thought of 'Nets' as being actually cricket. Track suits and ancient jumpers are the order of the day. They begin to play.

Their timing was perfect. Just as Piers was delivering the first ball the stadium erupted in a maelstrom of sound. An ear-assaulting barrage of music through which a voice could be heard bellowing.

"ONE ... TWO ... THREE ... FOUR ... ONE ... TWO . .. THREE ... FOUR."

The team stood still. Through the double doors, underneath the end balcony, a hundred and fifty nubile, beautiful girls appeared. Led by a macho instructor, who was the voice controlling the movements that matched the music. They filled the hall. For the complete hour that the cricket team attempted to practice they were accompanied by the music, the counting and the contorting bodies doing their aerobics to the loud, repetitive beat. The effect, on Piers in particular, was traumatic. For the rest of the season he could only bat to music. The solution proved to be a Walkman, which generally guaranteed him an innings until the end of the tape. This totally illegal use of a mechanical aid came to an end when a bouncer removed both the recording apparatus and half his left ear.

CHAPTER FOUR

The Indoor League

In which an 'Irresistible Force' meets an 'Immovable Object' and Piers remembers his prayers.

It was unfortunate that the Club's decision to enter the Indoor League coincided with Toby's major house move from one end of the village to the other. He duly notified the authorities of his new address and received an acknowledgement from the League Secretary; who continued to send all the post to his old address. Since the exchange of contracts on the houses had not been achieved without a certain degree of hostility, and despite having informed the Post Office of the change, a considerable number of letters went astray. These included details of the fixtures for the start of the season, with the result that by the time Toby realised what had been going wrong, Much Sloggin' by the Willow were unhappily in bottom place in the league, having apparently played three and failed to turn up for any of them. Letters of censure were sent to Toby's 'old' address. What was later to prove even more disastrous was that they had had no experience of the 'strategy' of the indoor game and had not even seen a match.

"Never mind," said Geoff, "it can't be that different, and there are still five games to play. If nothing else it will stand us in good stead for the coming season and give us some much needed practice before we start nets."

Toby made a visit to the Sports Hall and obtained a photo-copy of the games that they had to play and the times when they were expected. Unfortunately he didn't get a copy of the rules.

"There are two ways of scoring runs"

"Why are we due to play at seven-thirty and at nine o'clock?" said Winston in an aggrieved voice. "That means, as it's a Sunday, that we're going to be there until after closing time."

"I think it's because the innings are split in order to speed things up," said Piers. "One side bats and then there's a break to give one of the other games that's being played time to play their first innings. It also means that you don't have to wait while a change over is made. The next team on is ready and raring to go. That's what I've been told, although I've never seen a game."

On the strength of this sparse knowledge, Piers became the expert.

Since the sides comprised only six players the first match that was actually played was with a team selected by the committee. It consisted of the committee, Geoff, Winston, Lobby, Toby, Richard and Gary. On arrival they despatched Piers, who had been designated umpire, to find out what the form was and what they had to do. His garbled account led Geoff to bat first.

"There are two ways of scoring runs," said Piers. "Firstly by striking the ball so that it hits the walls. On either side that counts for a single. If you hit the wall behind the bowler that's a four if the ball goes in the air and a six if it's driven along the ground. If it hits the wall behind the wicket keeper that's two runs, so cuts and glides are worth cultivating. The second method of scoring is by running. Suppose you hit the ball against the side wall. That's a single. Then if you run as well that counts for an extra two."

There was a third method of scoring that Piers was unaware of since it hadn't been mentioned to him. If the bowler's line strayed at all from a line between the stumps then the umpires were very keen on raising their arms and shouting 'Wide' to the confused scorers.

The side against which the club were to make their debut seemed to consist entirely of teenagers.

"This is a bit of an insult," said Lobby. "I thought this was a proper adult league, what sort of a chance have these youngsters got against our experience?"

At seven-thirty sharp, the opposition were warming up and Geoff led his team to the corner of the hall, where they were to sit and wait their turn to bat. They were in fact on the playing surface, the boundary line in their corner being marked by a bench turned on its side. Situated at third man, it proved to be a dangerous area from two points of view. Both scorers sat there and had been known to come to blows; meanwhile the batsman's desire to edge fast bowlers in that direction meant compulsory watching of every ball.

Geoff decided to open with Richard and Toby. Richard's nickname wasn't 'Skuttle' for nothing. He had been known to steal singles before his batting partner was aware what was happening. It was unfortunate that Toby, peering through his glasses, had decided to play himself in without realising that Skuttle was backing up. A handsome squarish cut was being admired by its perpetrator when he became conscious of a figure next to him clutching a bat. There was no point in running but Toby had the good grace to move forward enough to put himself out of his ground; so that it was his wicket that was surrendered. He returned to his corner with the dignity of a Sydney Carlton muttering something about it being a far, far better thing if Richard did something unmentionable with his bat.

Field placing is important if you only have four men apart from the bowler and the wicket keeper. The opposition had acquired experience that belied their ages and were playing a classic two-two

"Richard's nickname wasn't 'Skuttle' for nothing."

field. Since real boundaries could only be scored on the wall behind the bowler there was a fielder at long off and another at long on. The remaining pair were both square with the wicket and positioned so that they could take both the direct shots and be in place for the rebounds. This proved to be doubly important when both Winston and Lobby were caught off the walls, an option they hadn't been aware of until it happened the first time. Two more run outs completed the innings and the final humiliating score was seventeen all out.

"I think that's a league if not a national record," said the opposition's scorer smugly. "We've now got an hour an a quarter before we can wrap this game up."

"What do you do in that time?" said Piers.

"Well, some of the team go for a swim and others go for an orange juice in the bar."

"The WHAT!" said Winston.

Three minutes later the committee were seated round a table clutching pints of anti-depressant Real Ale.

"Oh, by the way, I forgot to tell you," said Piers. "When a batsman reaches twenty-five runs he has to retire, but he can come back again if all the other wickets fall."

"Thanks Piers," said Toby, addressing his remarks to Skuttle. "If we'd known that I'm sure we'd have been more careful."

The next hour was the most pleasant of the evening. When the team returned to the hall they found that only three of their opponents were in the corner, alongside the scorer.

"Quickly, Winston," said Geoff. "Two wickets before the rest of the team arrive and we've won."

The umpire had other ideas. Four of the first five balls of Winston's first over were called wide, including one which nicked the inside edge of the opener's bat and, without deviating too much, bowled him middle stump.

Winston began to get cross. He walked down the wicket and, with great deliberation and restraint, marked two imaginary lines at the far end just in front of the batsman.

"I am going to pitch inside those," he said on his return to the umpire. "You will say nothing and your arms will stay by your sides."

"Turned up the following week completely kitted out in American football gear"

The next ball was straight and driven with tremendous force along the ground back towards Winston, who stuck out an enormous foot. The ball ricocheted to no man's land at mid wicket. Winston took off after it.

He was in full flight and just about up to his impressive maximum speed when he realised that although he would reach the ball before it hit the wall, there was nothing he could do to stop himself.

The noise of the impact caused all activity in the Sports Centre to stop. Winston dropped, the floor shook and he didn't move. Piers was the first to react. He rushed across from his position at square leg umpire and put his head on Winston's chest.

"He's dead," he screamed in a high soprano voice. Falling to his knees he clasped Winston's enormous hand between his own and began to pray.

Geoff and Roger arrived and kicked him out of the way.

Laboriously, with help, they got the giant to his feet and bent him double.

When he'd recovered he was able at last to speak.

"Hitting the wall and knocking myself out is nothing," he said. "To come round and find Bloody Piers praying in Latin is absolutely terrifying."

The game was the first of a string of five defeats.

The team, however, began to attract the largest crowds ever seen at an indoor cricket match. The reason was Winston. Following his painful experience in the first game he turned up the following week completely kitted out in American Football gear. Far from emulating the 'Refrigerator' he was more like an enormous oven on Gas Mark 9. The perspiration poured off him, causing one young lady spectator to faint. When revived she was heard to say:

"I thought he had melted."

He was, melting, creating an additional hazard as his sweat turned the floor into an ice rink.

This gave Geoff the important 'strategic' idea of always fielding first so that the opposition had the worst of the fielding conditions. Even this failed, since he lost the toss for the four remaining games, and was made to bat first every time.

Incidentally the scorer was right. Not only was the initial seventeen all out a league 'low', the end of season record of played eight, lost eight was also an all time worst.

CHAPTER FIVE

The 'Glory Hole'

In which the team dodge the April showers to assemble at the clubhouse and contemplate the contents of the 'Glory Hole'.

"Everybody here by eleven o'clock on Sunday." Geoff's instructions had been clear and there was a good response. Seven of the team had arrived by the time the bar was due to open. To be informed by Winston, as he dangled the keys, that he would unlock when the kitroom was cleared, sorted and the nets securely in place ready for the practice, due to take place that afternoon and then every Tuesday and Thursday.

'Kitroom' was a euphemistic term for the sanctuary which was Nathaniel's storeroom. The roof of which was adorned by what appeared to be fishing nets ... nets used with great enthusiasm during April and early May the previous season, what in fact had proved to be the summer before the rains came. Gathered in October by the group who turned up for 'maintenance'. The whole parcel, pegs, guy lines, wires and 'Holy Holy' nets had been bundled unceremoniously on top of the shed.
"Sooner we start," began Geoff.
"Right," said Roger. "The Glory Hole."
Gloryhole was right. The single bulb lit up a scene of total chaos. A corner into which everything had been thrown. Odd stumps, bails of ash, mahogany, oak and balsa wood (for the oppositions' innings) assorted straps, pads and gloves. On the two shelves reserved for the Cricket Club there was a more orderly pile. A pristine cardboard box, which when opened revealed a dozen new

"Nigel in the 'Glory Hole'"

balls, slightly mildewed, no longer valid for league games since the secretary obtained a new contract, or contact.

"Right," said Toby, spectacles on nose and notebook in hand. "Let's do a stocktake then we can see what we'll need for the season."

"Bats," said Nigel. "I hung them up last year to make sure they stayed in good condition."

Bats, the other variety, you would normally find hanging upside down in the darkest corner. Here, Nigel had gone mad with a ball of string, roping the handles together so that they hung in clusters with fronds of black and green tentacles hanging down, where the force of gravity had scraped the rotting rubber from the handles.

"We'll leave you to sort them out and report back," said Toby. "Take them outside and leave us some space."

Lobby had in the meantime been collecting the batting gloves together.

"There are four pairs here which are almost unused," he said, with a certain degree of awe.

"Marvellous," said Toby. "What are the markings inside them?"

There was a pause while Lobby put on his spectacles and moved to the doorway.

"Oh," he said. "L.H.C."

"No wonder they're untouched," said Toby. "Left handed Colts, since we only played three Junior fixtures last year."

"And only one of the team is left handed."

"Who bats at number eleven."

"Once, for two balls as I remember," said Geoff.

Lobby in the meantime had been collecting up the remaining gloves and moved outside to sort them.

Pads proved to be a real problem. There they lay, a strange watercolour mixture of grey and off white. The oldest sprouting a strange mixture of wiry hair that appeared to be growing; the newest, if the colour was anything to go by, leaking an ectoplasm of orange spongy foam. Over half the pads had faulty straps. It is one of life's problems that whenever there is a collapse in the batting order and a player rushes to put on a pair of pads; if indeed a pair can be found; that the last strap to be fastened is the one that is missing; or even worse, the pin from the buckle is missing, if the buckle itself is there. So the pads are torn off, another pair found and then the last strap hasn't got a hole in the right place. All this was to be corrected at this kit-sorting meeting. Which proved impossible since the final array of pads contained the results of previous seasons' numberings. They were all labelled: 32b; 40, 11a; 7; 23c. In addition some were lettered from years, and teams, gone by: M.S.V.; MUCH; M.C.C.; C.C.C.; P.C.; OLD P's. A motley assortment and not a real pair among them.

"What we're going to have to do," said Geoff. "Is clean the lot, make pairs out of them, scrub out the letters and numbers, whitewash the lot and start again. Winston, that's your job."

It was as well that Lobby was outside when they discovered the wicket-keeping gloves. There were three of them, on top of the paraffin heater. The red rubber palms had melted and they were locked together like shy mating octopuses who had been overtaken by an outside force which had welded them 'in flagrante delicto'.

The bag, empty, was discovered at the bottom of the pile. As with all ancient cricket bags it attacked two of the players with its rapier before the metal rod was pushed back into the solid leather strip at the top.

Empty it appeared to be, but closer inspection revealed a shocking pink, cricketer's box, with the initials, R.A.M.C., in blood red, across the front. Even more terrifying were the teeth marks round two of the edges.

"Weally, how disgusting. Whose is it?" asked Piers.

"This belonged to the great, and late, founder of the club," Geoff said, a serious, almost reverent look on his face.

"What happened to him?" said Piers.

A hint of a smile crossed Geoff's face. "You remember, Horatio, that little puppy we met last year?"

"Puppy!" said Piers. "That monster was the biggest Irish Wolfhound I've ever seen. He was heavier than Winston."

"You should have seen his great grandfather," said Geoff. "Our founder, God rest him." Those assembled crossed themselves. "Our founder was chased by Great Grandfather Horatio and caught in the allotments. By the time the police reached him all that was left was a pair of pads and that box you're holding."

Piers dropped the offending remnant as the other players collapsed in a helpless, laughing heap.

Some sort of an order was made out of the assembled bits and pieces and Toby retired with his list to work out what new kit they would need for the beginning of the season. Rumour had it that on the last occasion that he'd gone to the local Sports Shop, the proprietor, when he'd heard that he was from the Much Sloggin' by the Willow Cricket Club, had taken off the normal 10% discount and added on 20%. He'd reluctantly agreed to sell the bats at the right price provided that Toby didn't reveal where he had bought them.

After an intermission of fifteen minutes, when Winston opened the bar, the players attacked the next Herculean Task. Putting up the nets. Once they'd unravelled them, they made a fair stab at cobbling the holes together. This was done by weaving a piece of string round the outside of each hole and then pulling so that the holes disappeared in rucked-up gatherings.

They were joined at this point by Nathaniel's Y.T.S. assistant, a young lad called Wayne. Nathaniel had installed concrete bases for the posts which supported the nets; leaving Wayne to put down a similar 'holder' for the stumps. Lobby was the one who Wayne proudly showed his venture into acquiring building skills.

"What's this then?" said Lobby.

"It's to put the stumps in," said Wayne.

"Have you seen much cricket?" said Lobby.

"Never," said Wayne.

There's an eighteen inch span between these holes," said Lobby.

"That's right," said Wayne. "I was told they were nine inches apart."

"Two points," said Lobby. "First of all there should be nine inches between the outside stumps; secondly it wouldn't work anyway because the first time Winston bowled and hit the stumps they'd break off at the base."

Wayne's face began to assume the expression of a fast bowler who'd just been taken off.

"Never mind, young 'un," said Winston. "It's a lovely bit of concreting."

Wayne cheered up.

"I'm sure," said Winston, "You'll be able to dig it up in one piece and find a use for it."

"Wayne stops play"

CHAPTER SIX

'Marrieds' v. 'Singles'

Being the Tale of Lobby's Debut as captain, wherein he learns that eleven bodies make a team, while welding together an international force by introducing players from Ireland, New Zealand, the Far East and the Ladies Room.

"We've got a free Sunday the week after next," said Gary, the fixture secretary.

"What!" Winston was horrified, "I need the practice. Can't you fix up a game with the Club Cricket Conference?"

"I could try," said Gary, without too much enthusiasm. "But you remember what happened last time. A lot of travelling and a very heavy defeat."

"That was your fault," said Geoff. "You can't blame the Conference after you've told them we were able to put out a strong side."

"I thought we might try an internal fixture," said Gary. "Youngsters against the Crumblies, for example."

"That's no good," said Roger. "They'll run us off our feet. What about marrieds against singles?"

"That means the singles will be without a captain," said Gary. "They'll all want to do it and there isn't anyone capable."

"There's always Lobby. He's a bachelor." Geoff smiled as he thought of the club's real eccentric.

"Do you remember the night we went back to his house?" Roger turned to Geoff.

"When he insisted on cooking breakfast for the three of us. Only too well!"

"I've never seen anyone so surprised . . ."

"Eggs . . . eggs." The pair of them exploded with laughter. It was some time before they could be calmed down enough to tell the story.

"Lobby opened some wine and got a carton of eggs out of the fridge. He turned on the electric cooker and put this enormous frying pan on the hob. Then Geoff opened the curtains in the other room and made the mistake of making an inane remark about it being a beautiful dawn." Roger started laughing again, tears streaming down his face.

"It was. A real 'Shepherds' Warning'." said Geoff. "Ruined the Sunday fixture because it started raining at eleven and stopped on Wednesday. But at that moment, the sun was just about to climb over Lobby's beloved roses. It was beautiful."

Roger recovered and continued. "We stood there admiring the spectacle and raised our glasses, toasting the morning. Then we followed Lobby back into the kitchen. He very carefully cut three rounds of bread, put them on plates and broke the eggs into a jug."

"There was an explosion," said Geoff. "When he tipped the eggs into the frying pan, there was a bang, a blue flash and a puff of smoke. When it had cleared the pan was empty."

"I've never seen anyone so surprised," said Roger. "He just stood staring at the pan, then at the cooker then the floor. He turned to ask us something when the remains of one of the eggs detached itself from the ceiling and landed bang on the top of his cranium."

"And you know what a fine head of skin he's got," said Geoff. "After that he just stood there while eggs rained down on top of him."

The thought of Lobby, standing like Chicken Licken from the childhood tale, claiming that 'The sky is falling' was too much for the raconteurs and their audience and they emulated the eggs and fell about all over the place.

"Do you realise," said Gary, eventually. "This is the so-called responsible ancient you are suggesting as a captain for the 'singles' side?"

"Ah!" said Geoff. "Now you're talking cricket. That's different, besides we marrieds are going to need all the help we can get."

The nature of the fixture finally being decided, the committee, or rather those who were there, pinned up a notice on the board and added a list showing the composition of the two sides. There were two A. N. Others on the married team and three on the singles side. Who they would actually become on the day was left to the recruiting ability of the captains. The teams were:

MARRIEDS	*SINGLES*
GEOFF (Capt.)	LOBBY (Capt.)
ROGER	GARY
WINSTON	NIGEL
TOBY	PIERS
ARTHUR	RICHARD
BILL	REGGIE
BEN	DINGER BELL
ALBERT	YVETTE
NATHANIEL	A. N. OTHER
A. N. OTHER	A. N. OTHER
A. N. OTHER	A. N. OTHER

"Just a minute," said Toby, "There are two names there that I don't recognise. Who is Reggie and who is Dinger Bell?"

"They arrived last week," said Geoff. "While you were inexcusably away on honeymoon. Reggie was introduced to us by the opposition, who'd brought him along because he's about to move to the village. He's due to take an audition with R.A.D.A. Quite a character. Long haired, dressed like a refugee from an Oxfam Shop."

"He's already got a nickname," said Roger, "Rabbit-on Reggie. I've never heard anyone with so much to say. Even before the game started he'd entertained us on such topics as: the roles he'd like to play when he's finished drama school; the development of his bowling technique and the history of the pure cotton collarless shirt he'd bought for 15p from a jumble sale."

"His bowling action is fantastic," said Geoff. "If you accept that the meaning of fantastic is 'strangely weird'. Apparently he'd once heard a theatrical director instruct an actor:

'You are alone on stage at the beginning of the play. Don't move or speak until you get the first nervous reaction from the audience. Which will probably be a giggle.' "

Roger continued, "He transposed this to the cricket field. He would mark time, on the spot, increasing the speed and raising his knees until the batsman made an impatient gesture. Then and only then, he would run up with fast, tiny paces and deliver the ball while airborne, in the middle of the huge leap he took to complete his run-up."

"What about Dinger Bell?" said Toby.

"He turned up last week," said Roger. "Came into the changing room and asked if his team was playing. Winston said to him:

'You've got the wrong team on the wrong ground and probably the wrong date. But get changed anyway, we're one short.' "

"It turns out that he's a dentist from New Zealand," said Geoff. "He's in this country for a couple of years. He enjoyed his game and asked if he could join the club, shapes up well with the bat, might make a good number three."

The morning of the 'Matrimonial Match' dawned, the sun shone and the scene was one of perfect rural tranquillity. Ideal for a cricketing contest between two well matched teams who knew each others' methods and weaknesses well.

The married team had recruited two players from Albert's many friends. When he had retired from his position as head of the local village school, some three years earlier, there had been a massive turn out of ex-pupils. Two of these he had 'phoned and persuaded to turn out for what he called 'An Important Charity Game'. It was said of Albert that the real Crumblies of the club were those who hadn't been taught by him.

Lobby had also been successful, from a numerical point of view at least, and had filled the three vacant spots in his side. Geoff's fourteen-year-old son, Gavin, had, unknown to his father, been approached and agreed to play. Yvette had volunteered an Irishman called Patrick who she claimed was a good sport. The last place had been filled by Lobby while at a Chinese restaurant on Saturday night. Having informed the assembled eaters that he was now a captain twice over he had had number one son of the proprietor presented to him. His references were superb. He had once played, well, fielded for twenty minutes, on the Cricket Club Ground in Hong Kong. Lobby snapped him up and had ten percent taken off his bill.

Geoff and Lobby strolled out to the pitch to toss up. Accompanied by players from both sides, who wished to further their education in 'strategy' by being there when a new variation of Geoff's routine would be needed. They were disappointed. For the first time in living memory a straightforward toss took place.

"Heads," said Lobby.

"You're right," said Geoff. "I expect you'll want to bat, won't you?"

It was an attempt at a double bluff and they both knew it.

"Yes," said Lobby. "We'll bat."

Lobby was convinced that he had taken to the art of captaincy like a duck to water, unaware that there were times when the pond froze over and even the most elegant of fowls became sliding, slithering objects of ridicule.

The pitch proved to be a masterpiece. Since Nathaniel himself was playing, and wished to ensure his personal safety, he had produced a track which was so slow that Winston was reduced to tears after he'd attempted to dig in two very short bouncers and been pulled to fine leg by a grateful Piers.

It was a flourish by the graduate that was not to last long. Rumour had it that he had surrendered the significance of his birth sign, Virgo, the night before, on the very track they were now playing on, to an unknown lady, reputed to bear a strong resemblance to the wife of one of the opposition. It gave new meaning to the name 'popping crease' and partly explained the umpire's delight in being able to call 'wide ball'. Certainly when Piers was at the pertinent end his head took longer than usual to come up and he was eventually bowled while still searching the ground around him for some hidden sign. He departed with a smile on his face.

On an afternoon when the shadows were sharp and the fielding side more noted for their experience than their present ability, the unbetrothed made hay. Nigel made a rapid fifty and the New

Zealander a competent thirty-four. Both fell to Robert, one of Albert's friends who had been brought on by Geoff, more in despair than hope. He was a hop, skip and whip type of bowler who succeeded in making both batsmen cut straight into the gnarled hands of Ben as he half-crouched at first slip with his elbows on his knees.

With the score at 106 for 3, Geoff realised that his next bowling change was crucial. He decided to gamble and tossed the ball to Roger. Consultations about field placing resulted in a compromise between the conventional, five and four divided between the on and the off sides, to the controversial, seven and two, two men out and seven clustered too close to the bat for comfort.

"That," said Roger, "may not keep them on their toes but it should certainly keep them awake."

"He was a hop, skip and whip type of bowler"

The bowling action of the senior professional could have been taken from a coaching manual. A beautifully smooth approach to the wicket, perfect sideways on body at the final stride and classic follow through. The variation of length of delivery was just right, aimed at tantalizing the batsman into indecision about whether to play forward or back. There was a small snag, demonstrated by the first delivery which bisected the two close fielders on the off side. Direction. On his arrival at the wicket Roger appeared to suffer from a variety of vertigo (from the Latin = whirling) which made the location of the stumps at the other end a total mystery to him. Second slip acted as wicket keeper to the first ball, leg slip took the second diving to his left.

It was at this point that Geoff demonstrated his experience. He walked across and had a brief talk to Roger, then moved Winston to silly mid off. Winston crouched, Roger bowled and Gary's leg stump cartwheeled over Toby's shoulder. Toby was unconcerned. He had been pressganged into keeping because he had been adjudged to have missed the previous week's games without an adequate excuse. Since it was unsafe to wear his glasses he was keeping mainly by sound and good fortune.

The entrance of Lobby, claiming the captain's right to put himself in the key batting position, provoked a conference between Winston, Geoff and Roger.

"Let him get into double figures," said Winston. "That'll make his season and then we can all relax. If you get him out for a duck he'll sulk."

"Agreed," said Geoff. "Take it easy Roger, or I'll move Winston and you won't get another ball straight all afternoon."

"So that was the plan," said Winston. "You were sacrificing me in the hope that Roger wouldn't want to hurt me."

"Something like that," said Roger. "Though it was more the other way round. Geoff intimated that you might get a little bit annoyed if I bowled, successfully, at the back of your head."

The plan succeeded. Lobby was allowed to edge his way into his teens before Winston was recalled.

The rest of the innings was a mixture of comedy and pure farce. After Lobby had been granted the privilege of one of Winston's better balls, Richard played back too far to Roger, treading on his stumps and Reggie talked his way through seven singles before being run out while chatting to the wicket keeper. Patrick fulfilled Yvette's commendation by assuming that cricket was akin to shinty. As the ball was bowled gently to him he used his knowledge of the rules to rush down the wicket, arms and legs flailing and kicked the ball up into an arc from whence it was smashed into the air and caught by Nathaniel. The difference between the rules of shinty and the laws of cricket were still being explained to the Irishman at closing time. Gavin scored a splendid flat batted four off the last ball of an over before being given out L.B.W.; to Geoff's disgust and relief. Disgust at the decision and relief because he'd been talked into paying ten pence for each run his son scored.

A diplomatic 'ten per cent off' single was given to Fang Hi, before the field closed in round the lovely Yvette. Fielders clustered at short leg to share their appreciation of her shorts and volunteer assistance with pad adjustment and correction of stance. Edward, Albert's other recruit became the most unpopular member of the side when he caught the first ball to hit Yvette's bat.

The final score:

MARRIED XI

Name	Catch	Bowling	Runs
Nigel	ct. Ben	bowled Robert	51
Piers		bowled Winston	12
Dinger Bell	ct. Ben	bowled Robert	33
Richard	hit wkt.	bowled Roger	5
Gary		bowled Roger	0
Lobby		bowled Winston	14
Reggie		run out	7
Gavin		l.b.w. Winston	4
Patrick	ct. Nat.	bowled Roger	0
Fang Hi		not out	1
Yvette	ct. Ed.	bowled Roger	0
Extras			24
		Total	151

"Yvette, with Toby guarding the rear"

A discussion between Geoff and Roger at the interval, when they realised how thin the quality of their batting was, and how long the tail, resulted in Edward and Robert, the two friends of Albert, opening the innings.

Bill and Ben had volunteered to umpire for first ten overs.

"If we're not needed before then," Ben had said.

It soon became apparent that they might be.

The batsmen, being new, had not experienced the theatrical tactics of Reggie, with the result that the first ball whistled past Edward's off stump while he was still trying to discover if and when the bowler was actually going to allow him to play. The second, wide on the leg side, flicked his pad.

"How's that!" The appeal came from Fang Hi, followed by similar shouts from Patrick and Yvette, fielding together on the long leg boundary. There was also a chorus of agreement from the pavilion, where the assembled players still hadn't forgiven Edward for catching Yvette. Bill hesitated then raised his finger.

"Out," he said. "Next time remember you're a gentleman."

It was advice that Piers was to take to heart.

Arthur came in at number three. As press officer he was placed higher in the order than his ability promised. It was a way of ensuring that the games were reported in the local paper. For the same reason he was treated gently by the bowlers, Lobby having had a quiet word with Reggie and Dinger. A single nudged through the slips saw him off the mark.

Robert was not so lucky. Having impressed the connoisseurs with two almost identical off drives for consecutive fours, he hooked the ball towards Fang Hi, who caught it. This was a complete surprise since Fang Hi played cricket with the same blind faith that possessed his relatives driving cars in Hong Kong. He attempted to catch the ball by lining it up with his head; extending his arms, fully stretched as if signalling a wide, then snapping them together, relying on outside agencies to make sure that all three vital items arrived at the same point at the same time.

Toby was stumped by Lobby from the medium paced, straight up and down bowling of Dinger Bell. It wasn't really Toby's fault, he being distracted by the behaviour of Yvette and Patrick who'd been placed at long off for the second over and were using the sightscreen as a convenient place to nip behind, to renew and deepen their relationship of the previous evening.

Roger's batting reflected his bowling. He played a text book forward defensive stroke down the wrong line and was bowled first ball.

Lobby now found himself with conflicting loyalties. While he was enjoying his role as captain, he realised that he would not relish being responsible for the total destruction of the opposition, since he had more in common with them. They were his peers and his friends. He relaxed his grip, trying to make a game from a situation where the score stood at 9 for 4.

So he took both the wicket takers off. He told Reggie he was too expensive because he'd given way nine runs in only one over then assured Dinger he was protecting his average for him.

By the time he brought them back, both Geoff and Arthur were well established and the runs were flowing. They kept pace with each other, reaching their personal fifties in the same over.

At 123 for 4 the 'senior' side seemed to be heading for victory when Lobby decided to sacrifice Gavin, who promptly bowled his father round his legs with a perfectly flighted leg break.

"Well bowled," said Geoff. "At least you remember some things I've taught you."

As is often the case with partnerships, Arthur departed in the next over, although in controversial circumstances. Fang Hi had been followed by the ball during the earlier part of the innings and had made two unsuccessful attempts to catch the ball. This had resulted in two resounding blows to the face. He had then been fitted with a batsman's helmet to protect him from further injury.

Arthur hooked, Fang Hi clapped and missed but the ball stuck in the visor of the helmet. Toby, who was umpiring, gave him out. The resulting arguments in the bar later ranged over three possibilities:

1. The batsman should have been given five runs because the ball had struck an 'artificial aid'.
2. He was out. Look in the scorebook.
3. Not out, the ball was dead.

But that was yet to come; as far as the game was concerned the score was now 126 for 6.

Winston watched as Bill played out the rest of the over and then considered the position as the field changed over. He'd been told by Geoff to 'stay there', but he thought about the rest of the batting order and came to his own decision. When Gavin bowled he took two mighty steps down the wicket and hit one of the biggest sixes ever seen on the ground. As Gavin reached the delivery stride for the next ball, Winston started down the wicket and then as Gavin dropped the ball short Winston stepped back and pulled the ball to square leg. Fang Hi set off in hot pursuit and had just caught up with the ball when Lobby made a big mistake.

"Let it go" he shouted, impatient for a quick return that would catch Bill a pitches length behind Winston.

Fang Hi stopped in mid stoop and let the ball trickle over the boundary for four.

Winston had a less comfortable time for the next three balls, but survived two appeals for l.b.w., contenting himself with the thought that a single off the last ball would give him the bowling. He played Gavin's top spinner into the covers, called and ran.

"You're younger than me lad," said Bill, when Winston met him at the other end. "See if you can get back."

Winston swore, turned, took three paces and threw himself at the crease and lost.

"Hard luck, Winston," said Lobby, who had astounded everyone by catching the return and actually taking the bails off cleanly.

At 136 for 7 the scene was set for a gentle exhibition of telepathic calling and running between the twins, Bill and Ben. They were well on course, having scored over half the runs needed when they tried to amble through a gentle two off a straight drive. Yvette emerged from behind the sightscreen, picked up the ball and gave it to Patrick who threw down Ben's wicket. Bill was so upset he gave a return catch to the bowler next ball. 145 for 9.

"Last over," called Geoff, who had taken over as umpire.

Albert, it must be said, had, even in youth, been a classic number eleven; while Nathaniel was happiest at twelfth man.

The field clustered round the cheerful groundsman as he decided whether he was going to bat left or right handed. He settled, Reggie marked time, marked time, marked time. Eventually all the fielders were standing watching the bowler, who was waiting for

"Piers—gentleman or pillock?"

the moment when Nat reacted. He didn't. This seemed to destroy Reggie's accuracy and ball after ball was bowled wide of the off stump, to the complete indifference of the batsman and the fury of Lobby and the rest of the team.

"Last ball," called Geoff. A local rule he'd just made up.

Reggie high stepped through his run, the ball came straight. Nathaniel didn't move. The ball hit his bat and curved in a gentle arc towards Piers, who positioned himself perfectly, cupped his hands in the classic manner and allowed the ball to fall through them. Thus proving to half the players involved in the day's struggle what a gentleman he was; and to the other half that he was a right pillock.

CHAPTER SEVEN

Venez a 'Plus Frappez Par Le Seule'

It rained for nine days in July. Four Saturdays and five Sundays. In between it drizzled.

Puddles formed on the top of puddles.

The sightscreen at the lower end of the ground, securely chained to an ancient and very heavy oak seat, was washed away. It followed the course of the local brook to the river and, breaking its journey only to win a prize in a fancy dress regatta at Henley, was last seen steaming down the English Channel proudly displaying Nathaniel's advertising campaign on its reverse side. When informed the entrepreneurial groundsman regretted the missed opportunity.

"Just think," he said. "I could have used French ... two languages ... and it was seen on television!"
"What would you have put on it?" said Winston.
"That's easy," said Nathaniel.

"Venez a 'Plus Frappez Par Le Saule'."

"Où," said Piers, "Il pleut ... et il pleut ... et il pleut."

"Il pleut"

CHAPTER EIGHT

The Visit of the Touring Celebrity side

In which the Much Sloggin' by the Willow Cricket Club is honoured by the visit of a touring Celebrity side, 'George's Marauders', an interesting mix of retired county second team players, local radio sports commentators and a television personality.

The first shock to the home side was the discussion Geoff had on the way to the wicket to flip his lucky Victorian penny.

"No need to toss up, is there?" said George the visiting captain. "My boys have found out that the bar is open all afternoon and there's no way they'd agree to field."

"Sure," said Geoff. "No problem. Tea at four thirty?"

"Between the innings," said George. "We'll aim at a score of 250 and then we'll let you get reasonably close. Don't worry."

The second shock was the one delivered to Winston. He had been looking forward to bowling to 'Batsmen of Quality', as he'd called them the previous evening.

"It will give me some idea of how good I really am. If I can keep them contained and perhaps take a wicket or two then the local sides will perhaps treat me with more respect."

He was loosening up outside the pavilion when one of the opening batsmen, known for his occasional appearances for the County First XI a decade or so previously, approached him.

"Listen, son," the old pro began, taking Winston's arm and leading him round the corner to a quiet spot. "They've come to see me not you. Play the game and pitch the ball up, just on a length and outside the off stump."

"They've come to see me, not you."

Winston consulted Geoff as they took the field.

"What should I do, skipper?"

Geoff was becoming a little overawed by the occasion.

"Well," he said, "You can dig one in at him and make yourself into a local hero, but there will no doubt be an unpleasant atmosphere after the game and I doubt whether we'd get the fixture again. Or you can do as you've been asked and let him make a few runs."

Winston complied. Fourteen runs came off his first over. Reggie from the other end faired little better and it soon became obvious that they were in for a hard day in the field.

Except Piers that is. He tried to get a too close look at the opener's technique and had to be rushed to the local casualty department to have five stitches put in a cut just above his eyebrow. There was a lack of sympathy on his return.

"While you were there," said Roger. "Did they give you an eye test?"

"No," Piers was confused. "Should they have done?"

"Well, you didn't catch the ball did you?"

The opposing captain was as good as his word. Although it did mean that tea was delayed until a quarter past five. The declaration came at 264 for 6, with the opener still there on 153 not out.

Piers and Nigel were allowed to make a good start, the fifty coming up in fairly quick time. Then wickets started to tumble, until Winston arrived at the crease and hit a magnificent career best 64. With the score at 193 for 9, and Geoff, who'd been in for an hour, protecting Reggie, there was a flurry of activity in the clubhouse. The opposition's scorer was taking bets that the score wouldn't reach 200. Geoff was facing and there were seven balls to go so it looked like a fair bet. Later it was suspected that this was an arrangement between George and the scorer to cover the evening's drinks bill. It certainly sucked in enough of the home team and supporters to add considerable interest to the rest of the innings.

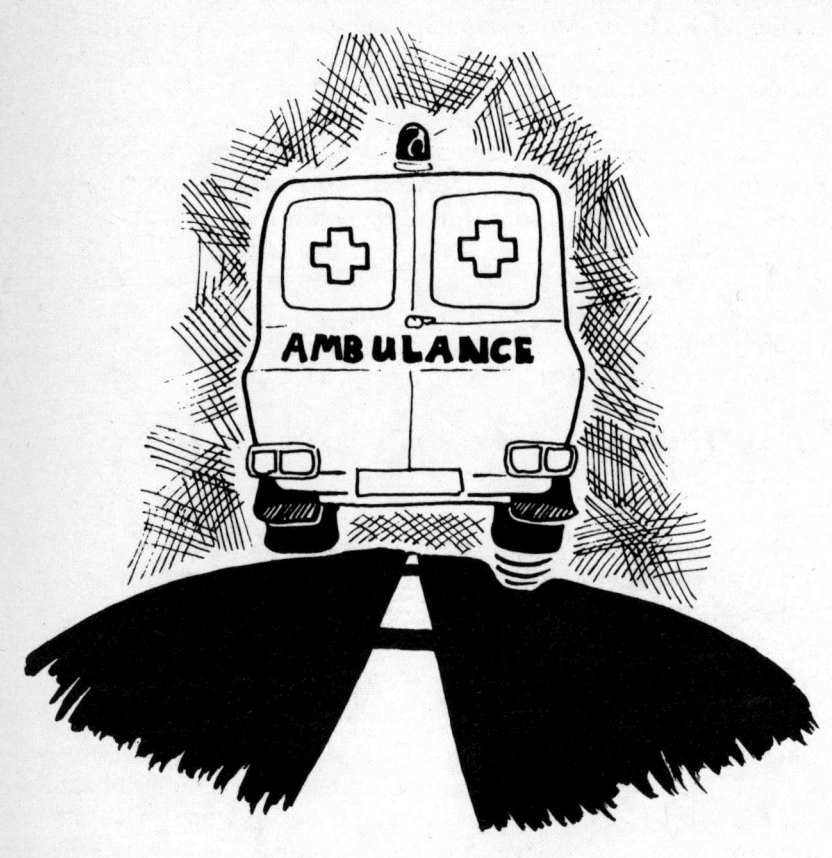

"Rushed to the local casualty department"

On the last ball of the penultimate over Geoff stroked the ball through the covers. The batsmen ran three and stopped, to make sure that Geoff kept the bowling. The fielder, seeing what had happened, kicked the ball over the boundary and signalled four, to enable the opening bowler to have a go at Reggie. Fortunately Ben was umpiring at the right end and he raised his hand and his voice, shouting to the scorer.

"Seven. Three and four overthrows."

Geoff played out the last over to leave the club at 200 for 9, the game as an acceptable honourable draw and the scorer paying off the happy punters.

CHAPTER NINE

The Ultimate in Local Derbies

Much Sloggin' by the Willow play their local rivals in the final of the Hospital Memorial Knock Out Cup.

The rules of the competition ensured that there would not be a home advantage. Essential since the 'art' of doctoring wickets had been perfected by local groundsmen. This, added to the unfailing 'strategy' of captains, combined to make the route to the final partly dependent on where the games were played. Much Sloggin' were in the final courtesy of a string of wins, resulting from their name being first out of the hat, in every round, when the draw for ground advantage was made.

So the final was to be played on the lush, plushly appointed, neutral ground of the top club in the next county. Indeed the luxury and newness of the clubhouse posed a major problem for the diminutive Lobby.

"Quick," he said, rushing into the bar area. "Come with me." He grabbed hold of Bill and Ben and dragged them from the room.

"Look at that," he continued, as they reached the toilets. "That is a travesty."

Bill and Ben were bewildered.

Lobby demonstrated.

When the gentle giants had stopped laughing they positioned themselves one either side of Lobby and lifted him up, so that he could reach, with comfort, the wall-mounted, china 'pissoirs' which had been fixed too high for those whose personal accessories were, relatively speaking, too close to the ground.

"For those whose personal accessories were too close to the ground"

The rules of the competition were fairly simple. Twenty overs for each side, no bowler to bowl more than four, with the result that at least five bowlers had to be used and the captains had to keep a careful check on who was going to bowl from which end. The alternative result would be that there would be overs in hand for the best bowler who would be unable to bowl from both ends!

The Indian Summer that they'd been enjoying meant that the track was dry and hard. As they examined it, Geoff and Roger reflected on tactics.

"We're going to have to rely on luck," said Geoff. "The real spin of the coin on this occasion. I'm too well known by Dave, Oving's captain, to be able to use any of the classic strategy."

"It looks to me to be a good toss to lose," said Roger, "I wouldn't want the decision of whether to bat or field. The wicket looks to be an ideal batting track but there's more than a touch of grass on it. Besides which, in this tournament, the side batting second and chasing are usually favourites. Balance that against a deterioration in the light towards the end of the game and it could be anyone's guess. All in all we'd be better fielding first."

Geoff smiled. "Suppose I come out with Dave and say to him . . . 'No need to toss up, you choose.' What do you think he'd say?"

"Might just throw him," said Roger. "Worth a try anyway."

When the time came Dave took a coin out of his pocket.

"No need to bother with that," said Geoff. "You can decide, what do you want to do?"

Dave was horrified.

"I'm not choosing," he said, "I want to toss up properly."

"But I'm saying that I don't want to, you can take it that you've won the toss. Now what do you want to do, bat first?"

"This is just another of your tricks," said Dave. "I insist that we toss up."

"Alright," said Geoff. "Let's toss up to see who doesn't have to make the decision. If I win the toss then I can ask you to choose. If you win then you can insist that I do. Agreed?"

Dave was, by this time, sufficiently confused to agree to almost anything, so he spun the coin high in the air.

"Heads," said Geoff.

"Gave the impression of being slightly vague"

"You're right," said Dave.

"We'll field," said Geoff.

"But you said . . ."

"That if I won the toss I could ask you to choose. I've decided to spare you the responsibility."

"But . . ."

Winston and Reggie were magnificent. After six overs the cream of the opposition's batting was back in the chrome and plastic comfort of the clubhouse. The score an encouraging 17 for 5. Even Bill and Ben, who had been dropped for the final in favour of the younger element, managed to smile.

Geoff decided to hold both his opening bowlers back for the final overs and brought on Roger and Dinger Bell. It was a brave move, but it proved to be expensive. Roger was having one of his days when the direction finder wasn't working. Lobby flung himself all over the place to save the byes but could do nothing about the wides, which the neutral umpire was signalling with all the enthusiasm of a boastful angler. Two overs were enough for the opposition and too much for Geoff. In the meantime at the other end Dinger was producing balls of immaculate direction but with a disastrous variety of length. The lower middle order batsmen gratefully accepted and despatched the loose balls through the many gaps in the field. Four disastrous overs had added thirty-one to the total.

Nigel was summoned. He was a bowler of undoubted class, who, to the uninformed spectator, might give the impression of being distinctly vague. This was in fact due to intermittent diabetes. The team had first become aware of this during a match they were playing at a Sports Complex covering many acres. There, a series of pitches almost overlapping in a myriad of ways and keenly contested games took place at the same time. Nigel having 'phased out' was discovered fielding in the wrong game, not just on the next pitch but three complete tracks away. He was doubly confused because the opening batsman in the first game had been out too quickly and had gone in number three in the next game, only to be bowled and appear at number five in the game where Nigel was eventually discovered. An early helping of the cake served for tea had sorted Nigel out on that occasion and the teams had learned to carry mini-Mars bars to straighten him out whenever he did a 'Wobbly'.

Suitably fortified by a generous chocolate ration he justified his captain's faith in him by bowling four immaculate overs during the course of which he took two wickets, at the economical cost of eleven runs.

Piers, brought on at the other end, kept a good line and length, taking a wicket with the last ball of his third over. This proved to be a mistake. He suffered from a distinct lack of respect from the opposition's number ten, who wasted no time in trying to read Piers distinct change of action when he switched from his carefully controlled off breaks, to the 'arm ball' which he loved to bowl. In his final over he was hit for two towering sixes over mid-wicket and finished with figures of 1 for 28 from his four overs.

Geoff was now in the happy position of having one over each left from Winston and 'Rabbit-on' Reggie. The score stood at 87 for 8 and there were two tail enders for them to bowl at ... albeit one who was top scorer by virtue of his savage attack on Piers. As he was facing, Geoff chose to give the penultimate over to Winston.

The first ball removed the batsman's off stump. Winston turned and, wrapping his enormous arms around the umpire, pinned his arms to his side, lifted him off his feet and kissed him on the forehead. The look of terror on the man's face testified to his courage or foolishness when, on his release, his right arm came out horizontally from his shoulder as he whispered 'No Ball' in the general direction of the scorer.

Winston's next ball caused the batsman to duck. The ball passed under his chin, removed part of the left side of Lobby's moustache and reached the boundary for four byes, first bounce. The next violated, for the second time, the golden rule relating to a fast bowler bowling to a fast bowler. Dug in short it reared and hit the batsman, who had foolishly continued his policy of 'swing and be damned', on his right eyebrow. He was rushed to hospital to be stitched up.

There are still tail enders who know their places. The incoming number eleven was a case in point. He took a leg stump guard, stepped back a further foot and was obviously thankful to be bowled first ball.

"Four point six an over," said Gary, the team's statistician, commenting on the target of ninety-two.

"Piers and Nigel are capable of getting the runs before we need to get worried about the scoring rate," said Geoff. "Especially now they're a bowler short."

Unfortunately nobody checked on Nigel's chocolate supply. He had been more active than usual, having distinguished himself with his four overs. Full of euphoria he forgot to supplement his thigh pad with the customary mini-Mars.

In the second over Nigel played an immaculate forward defensive stroke, allowing the ball to hit the bat and stop directly in front of him. As there was no fielder within fifteen yards of him he stooped down, picked up the ball and lobbed it back to the bowler. Piers, in the meantime, had called for a quick single and was racing down the pitch. The bowler grinned and removed the bails. Piers comment to Nigel owed a great deal to the foreign languages that he had studied before going to university.

Two balls later Nigel was bowled, playing down the wrong line. He later claimed to be attempting to move cover point.

Dinger and Roger then settled down for the next four overs, keeping their heads down and trying to bring some stability to the innings. Gary paced the boundary, groaning to himself as the run rate slipped further and further behind. A double bowling change enabled Dinger to open up the game with some classic off drives, while Roger contented himself with the occasional nudge to leg. The fifty came up in the fourteenth over. Gary was heard to mumble that seven an over was possible.

The opposition's skipper faced with having to find two more bowlers, at least, gambled on bringing his opener back for his final over. The third ball had just been beautifully square cut for four by the New Zealander, when there was a screech of brakes and a slamming of doors from the car park.

The car park is situated at a lower level than the ground. The first glimpse of the noisy passengers was the appearance of a blood-stained bandage as the 'casualty' mounted the steps by the side of the pavilion. Disturbing brown stains could be seen on the shirt of the apparition as he made his way to the boundary rope and stood watching Dinger take six more runs off the remainder of the over. He then walked to the wicket, talked to his captain and peeled off his sweater.

The first two balls gave an indication of what was to come. Roger just managed to get his bat down on the swinging yorker as it pitched in the blockhole. The second lifted off a length and left Roger wondering what had happened to it. It had in fact flicked the shoulder of his bat and flown high over third man for six. The third ball was just short, dug well in and on its way to bury itself in Roger's rib cage when he managed to fend it off . . . only to be caught at forward short leg.

Geoff decided that advanced 'strategy' was called for and asked for leg stump. He then stopped the bowler half way down his run up and called to the umpire.

"I think I'd better change my guard. Leg stump doesn't really get my body behind the ball. Give me centre and I'll shuffle across. Sorry bowler."

True to his intent Geoff moved across and played the leg glance so beloved of Indian Princes. Unfortunately the stroke was played after the ball had removed his leg stump.

Lobby, realising that he was likely to be the final part of a hat trick, pulled himself up to his full height. Towering head and shoulders above the stumps he stood prepared to do battle. The bowler produced the most vicious ball he had bowled so far. Lobby ducked into it and there was a sound reminiscent of two snooker balls, impacting at full speed, as the dome of the diminutive wicket keeper's head took the full impact. He dropped, pole-axed.

It took a good five minutes to bring him round. Resisting all entreaties to leave the field he was eventually spoken to by the umpire.

"Are you fit enough to walk?"

"Yes," said Lobby, gritting his teeth.

"Then start walking. You're out L.B.W."

Toby survived the last ball of the over.

Back in the pavilion Geoff called a conference.

"Look," he said to the remaining batsmen. "There are four overs left. The other opening bowler will probably be asked to take his final one now to keep the pressure on us. Bloody Nelson has two to come from his end but in between there has got to be an over from a sixth bowler and that's where our main chance must be. Here's what you've got to do. Defend. Just look for a chance to take a single and give Dinger the bowling. Take no chances and he can win the game. Got it?"

There was universal agreement.

The first part of the prediction proved to be correct. The second opening bowler returned and was promptly hit for two fours by Dinger. An off drive from the third ball looked a certain two until Toby slipped and they had to be content with a single. The fourth ball found the edge of his bat and was gratefully pouched by the wicket keeper.

Richard had listened to Geoff's advice but not really thought the strategy through. On managing to connect with the first ball he

"Nelson"

"They departed in a taxi"

received, a Chinese cut to fine leg, he set off with the intention of giving Dinger the bowling, totally oblivious to the fact that there was only one ball to go. The opening bowler produced his better ball which Dinger couldn't score from, and Richard found himself facing the prospect of six balls from 'Nelson'. He was half way into a modest backlift when he heard the stumps clatter behind him. Gary was far more successful. He succeeded in hitting the ball, hard, straight back at the bloodied bowler who hung on to it as it thudded into his body.

Enter Winston.

As he stood taking his guard from the umpire, the bowler walked down the track and stood toe to toe with Winston, staring him in the eyes with his one good eye, as malevolently as a heavyweight boxer trying to out-psyche his opponent.
"I'm just picking the spot," he said and marched back to his mark.
Winston knew what to expect. Geoff's instructions were going over and over in his brain . . . 'A single, get a single. Give Dinger the bowling.'
The next three balls were delivered with as much venom as 'Nelson' could muster. Criminally short they were accurately directed at Winston's left eyebrow.
All three were flat batted over mid-wicket for successive sixes as Winston stood up and swung.

The game was over.

Geoff, Roger, Lobby and Winston drank six pints, each, before thinking about changing out of their whites. They then decided that it wasn't worth the effort and continued the celebrations until they were thrown out at closing time, when they departed in a taxi.

At six o'clock the following morning Richard was woken up by the persistent ringing of the telephone. He answered it with difficulty.

"Can you meet us at the station?"

"Will you accept a transfer charge call from a Mr Winston Garfield Dubois Smith?" The disembodied voice was sceptical to the point of disbelief. This was obviously a send-up.

Richard's brain struggled to activate his tongue.

"Yes."

"Richard. It's Winston."

"Yes."

"I'm with Geoff, Roger and Lobby."

"Yes."

"Can you meet us at the station at a quarter to seven?"

"Tonight?"

"No. This morning."

"Why?"

"Well. You're the treasurer."

"So . . ."

"We've just woken up at Waterloo Station and we need someone to meet us and pay our fares."

CHAPTER TEN

The Annual Dinner Dance

Guest Speaker, Pieter Van Schwarzwinkel from Cape Town and the County First XI. The raffle for the Autographed Cricket Bat.

"This year," said Winston, "I am going to make sure that peace and harmony reign at our Dinner Dance. There is going to be no excessive drinking and we shall all part friends at the end of the evening."

Geoff interrupted. "Why should this year be any different?"

"Because I have guaranteed the owners of the hotel that there will be no repetition of last season's disgraceful scenes in the car park. Besides which, I do not have the funds to pay off outraged local residents for damage to their garden gnomes."

The committee were putting the final touches to the arrangements for the prestigious end of the season social event, to be held the following Saturday. The guest speaker, enjoying a benefit year with the County, had been persuaded into attending yet another rural outpost with the promise of a minimum fee and possible extra fund-raising support. The 'entertainment' had been booked and the hotel assured that all would be well.

"Any other problems?" said Winston.

"Yes," said Richard. "As treasurer of the club I look forward to receiving a credit for our funds at the end of the event rather than a bill. I hope the Dinner Dance sub-committee will keep that in mind."

"This is not a money making event," said Winston. "It's a night to wind up the season, present the odd award, listen to the guest speaker and dance. And there isn't a sub-committee. I'm in charge."

Silence. Winston was not to be argued with when in command, besides which no one in their right mind would want to be co-opted on to any event with money involved.

Cometh the night. The gathering in the bar was a classic. The ladies were seated in their social groups sipping their exotic cocktails (an innovation introduced by Winston, after consultation with his wife), while the men grouped at the bar downing pints with the speed of those convinced that the supply was about to run out.

Pieter van Schwarzwinkel, the guest speaker, arrived at eight o'clock, just in time to be introduced to Geoff and Carole, Winston and Tallulah and Lobby before taking his place with them at the 'High' table.

It was a noisy meal. The food had been selected by the committee, in consultation with the hotel chef. Flair and haute

"The Y.T.S. youth who had to be helped by Nathaniel"

cuisine had been abandoned for the traditional 'club' menu of Prawn Cocktail, Gammon Steak with Pineapple, Black Forest Gateaux and Cheese and Biscuits.

The wine waiter had a hard time. Due to the illness of the professional the job was undertaken by a ingénue Y.T.S. youth who failed to master the complexities of the double-handled, cork extractor and had to be helped by Nathaniel, whose experience with the tractor stood him in good stead. The wine flowed. The cellar's supply of Liebfraumilch and Spanish Red was soon exhausted and progress made down the wine list with aplomb varying from the expert to the thirsty.

"A bottle of number seventeen. That's the eighty-three Chablis."

"Two of those over here, and one of the big red ones they've got on the top table."

It was later claimed that it was Lobby's idea to order the port, mainly because he happened to be talking about mess dinners and the importance of passing the decanters the right way. Although he denied it, the cost was added to his bill, which Winston had to pay for him. The dignity of the ritual was slightly disrupted when two of the ladies wanted lemonade to go with their port.

"Ladies and Gentlemen," Lobby made his first attempt to gain the attention of the gathering.

"Sing us a song!" The raucous shout from the lips of the demure Piers brought the assembly to instant silence. He turned bright red, looked round at the sea of faces staring at him and slid quietly under the table, where he was used as a foot rest by his team mates.

"Our guest speaker for the evening," said Lobby, making full use of the temporary lull. "Needs no introduction from me. The five centuries he has scored for the county speak for themselves. I give you ... Pieter van Schwarzwinkel."

The star stood up and smiled. Apart from batting it was the thing he did best. As an after-dinner speaker he was a total disaster. The final message was that he was only in cricket for the money and since there wasn't enough in England he was only going to play in Australia in the future.

The applause was polite and muted.

"If I could have my cheque now," Pieter van Schwarzwinkel said, "I have two more meetings to get to tonight."

"The star stood up and smiled"

He left.

"Awards," said Lobby, holding up two statuettes. "Clubman of the year, presented by Nathaniel Whorethorn, the club's 'Ground Superintendent'. This handsome trophy goes to the person who has contributed most to the growth of Much Sloggin' by the Willow Cricket Club. This year the winner is . . . Nathaniel Whorethorn."

Nathaniel was sufficiently overcome to be rendered temporarily speechless.

"The second handsome extra award, kindly presented by our captain, Geoff, is for the most promising newcomer. This goes to Gavin, Geoff's son."

Winston rose to his feet.

"You are now at liberty to refresh your drinks at the bar. Raffle tickets for the autographed bat will be on sale. The entertainment will commence at eleven o'clock to be followed by the draw for the bat."

Music was being provided by a punk-haired D.J. with a mind-bending lighting display and speakers the size of wardrobes. A cacophony of hard rock ensured that the floor was not used for the first half an hour. The only performance came from the gyrations of the youth changing the records. Then a Rolling Stones record changed the entire scene. It became obvious that the over-forties ruled. Or so they thought. Once the sixties' sound had been established, the younger element adopted it as their own and the floor was soon a mass of heaving, twisting, rock and roll enthusiasts. Bill Bailey may not have come home but Bill Haley was alive and well and moving.

Part of the tradition of the annual dinner dance was that there should be a break in the dancing while the 'choice' of the committee performed. This usually took the form of a double act who sang solos and duets from the hit parade and told a few harmless stories . . . turquoise rather than blue.

This year the choice had been left to Winston. He had accepted the recommendation of some of his workmates and booked Paul and Pauline, sight unseen.

He had not expected, or would ever live down, the floor show that followed. Even a stripper would have had an appeal to half the audience . . . but a pair of elderly transvestites, in a routine that

"Toby, standing between Tallulah and Carole"

involved revealing all to the strains of 'Beautiful Dreamer', would have strained the tolerance of a more sober audience.

A veil, which would have helped the performance, drawn over the proceedings is the kindest act we can achieve.

Tallulah did not speak to Winston for two weeks.

The organisation of the raffle for the bat was in the safe hands of the myopic secretary, Toby. The prize had been the idea of the Ladies' Committee who bought the bat and arranged for it to be autographed by the players from the visiting celebrity side. The prize had been guarded at a secret location by Tallulah and was produced, in its leather sheath, as the moment for the draw drew near.

Talulah and Carole assisted Toby with mixing the raffle tickets in the tub provided by the hotel. There was a great deal of giggling between the ladies which left Toby looking even more bewildered than usual. He was invited to pick the important number. Standing between Tallulah and Carole he reached up to the container held just above his head and stirred . . . stirred . . . stirred. Expectation was replaced by impatience.

"Hurry up you silly old sod."

"They'll catch fire in a minute."

"What have you got in there?"

Toby prevaricated, relented, pulled out a ticket and handed it to Tallulah.

"The winner is . . . blue ticket . . .number one hundred and three."

There was a rustling of paper as heads went down, checking.

"It's mine! It's mine!"

The voice came from the back of the hall and a figure came rushing between the tables and up on to the stage.

It was Nathaniel.

"I can use it, I can use it."

"What's he talking about, he only bats once a year," said a disgruntled voice.

"Just think of the advertising," said Nathaniel. "I could put it on display and charge admission."

Tallulah and Carole dissolved in uncontrollable laughter.

Toby presented the prize and Nathaniel lovingly removed the bat from its protective covering, then held it up for everyone to see. It was covered in signatures.

"There are more here than just the one team," he said. Then looked closer.

"With love from Tallulah," he read in a halting voice.

"I'll always remember you, Carole."

"You're the greatest, Samantha."

"Yours, Yvette."

Toby led him from the stage and back to his place.

It transpired that the Ladies Committee had decided that their signatures were far more important than those of a once seen visiting team and had agreed to do the honours themselves.

"It's unique," said Tallulah, as Nathaniel cheered up. "Unlike the County ones which are two a penny, there is only one like this in the whole world."